CHAPTER 1: INTRODUCTION

Welcome

Hello and welcome to *Run Your First 10K: A Step-by-Step Beginner's Guide from Couch to Confident Finisher*! You're about to embark on an exciting new challenge, and whether you're starting fresh from the couch or ready to take on a new distance after completing a 5K, this book is here to guide you to the 10K finish line with confidence.

The Spirit of the Torch Race

In ancient Greek games, there was a race called the Lampadedromia, or Torch Race. The winner wasn't the fastest but the one who reached the end with their flame still burning. It was about endurance and resilience—keeping the flame alive.

As you begin your journey to 10K, let this story be your guide. Reaching the finish line isn't about being the fastest or perfecting every step; it's about staying consistent, finding your rhythm, and keeping your own flame—your motivation and determination—alive. Together, we'll make that finish line a reality, one step at a time.

The Benefits of Running a 10K

Before diving into the benefits, understand that running a 10K positively impacts your physical and mental well-being.

1. **Building Exceptional Cardiovascular Fitness**
   With each run, you're strengthening your heart, increasing lung capacity, and improving circulation. These benefits bring more energy to every part of your life, helping you feel more vital and energetic every day.
2. **Developing Mental Resilience**
   Training for a 10K is as much about building the mind as it is the body. With each mile, you'll learn to overcome moments of doubt, push through discomfort, and discover your inner strength. This resilience isn't limited to running—it's something you carry with you, ready to apply in other areas of life.
3. **Strengthening Muscles and Joints**
   A 10K encourages a balanced approach to training that includes both strength and flexibility, which protects your body from injury and builds a foundation for longer runs. You'll develop leg strength, core stability, and flexibility, all of which support your overall fitness.
4. **Encouraging Consistency and Healthy Habits**
   As you progress through this program, you'll find yourself developing a routine that helps you stay focused and committed. Running becomes more than a goal—it's a lifestyle that supports long-term health and well-being.
5. **Achieving a Profound Sense of Accomplishment**
   Reaching the 10K finish line, whether in an organized race or on your own, fills you with pride. I remember Sarah, one of my first running partners, who completed her first 10K after starting with brief jogging intervals. The joy on her face as she crossed the finish line was proof that she had overcome her doubts and achieved something meaningful. You'll have proved to yourself that you're capable of achieving something truly meaningful, and that feeling will stay with you long after the race is over.

Why I Wrote This Book

Running has given me a stronger body, a resilient mind, and a deep sense of fulfillment. I wrote this book to help others experience that same joy and achievement.

Whether you're coming to this journey fresh or building on a 5K foundation, *Run Your First 10K* is crafted as a Complete 10K Training Guide. It provides all the tools, insights, and support you'll need to succeed. My goal is that this book becomes not just a training plan but a companion through every stage of your journey. It's here to encourage you on the challenging days, celebrate with you as you progress, and remind you of the strength you're building, one run at a time.

The road to 10K is yours. Like the torchbearers of ancient Greece, you're setting out to reach the finish line with your flame still burning strong. I'm honored to be a part of your journey. Let's take it one step at a time, from the couch to the finish line. Set a date for your first 10K, sign up for a local race today, and consider joining a local running community or online group for additional support and motivation.

CHAPTER 2: GETTING STARTED

Assessing Your Current Fitness Level

As you begin your 10K journey, the first step is assessing your current fitness level. Each runner starts from a different place, and that's perfectly okay. No matter where you are now, this chapter will help you create a realistic starting point.

If you're completely new to running, it can be helpful to start with short intervals—combining walking with brief jogs to build a foundation of stamina and confidence. Begin with intervals that feel manageable. For example, try alternating 1 minute of running with 3 minutes of walking. Repeat this cycle for about 20–30 minutes, and gradually increase the running intervals over time.

If you've already completed a 5K, your foundation is solid, and you're ready to build on that strength. You can start with longer runs at a comfortable pace, focusing on maintaining a steady rhythm rather than speed. Gauge how you feel during these runs; if they feel good, you're ready to begin the 10K program. If they feel too challenging, pull back slightly and work up to a comfortable pace before diving into the next level.

Assessing your fitness is about understanding what feels right for you, and each step forward builds a stronger foundation.

Setting Goals

Setting goals helps keep you motivated and on track. Whether it's completing a 10K or achieving a personal time milestone, make your goal inspiring yet achievable to stay challenged without feeling overwhelmed.

In my experience, breaking goals down into smaller milestones makes the journey more enjoyable and achievable. For instance, if you're aiming to run the 10K without stopping, set mini-goals like completing a 3K without stopping first, then progressing to 5K, and so on. Celebrating each of these small victories builds confidence and motivation.

If you're an experienced runner and aiming to beat a specific time, focus on incremental improvements. Setting a goal of shaving off one minute over two weeks, for example, gives you something tangible to work toward while preventing burnout.

Remember, goals are there to guide you, not pressure you. Celebrate each milestone, no matter how small, and recognize every step forward as a win.

Mindset Matters

Running is just as much a mental journey as it is physical. Building mental resilience has been essential in my progress, especially on days when motivation was low. On some days, it's easy to lace up and head out the door, while on others, it's hard to even get started. That's when mindset becomes your best ally.

A big part of building resilience is learning to appreciate small wins and not getting discouraged by setbacks. If you have a tough run, focus on what you accomplished rather than what didn't go as planned. Each challenging run builds mental strength and brings you closer to your goal.

Staying positive often comes down to shifting your perspective. Instead of viewing tough runs as struggles, see them as opportunities to grow stronger. When self-doubt creeps in, remind yourself why you started and what finishing this 10K will mean to you. Each step forward is progress, and every challenge

TOMASZ TOMASZEWSKI

adds to your resilience.

CHAPTER 3: 10K TRAINING PLAN

Overview of the 8-Week 10K Training Program

This 8-week program is designed to guide both beginners and more experienced runners through a balanced and sustainable 10K training journey. There are two tracks: one for beginners starting from scratch and another for intermediate runners who've completed a shorter distance like a 5K. This plan focuses on building stamina and endurance gradually while prioritizing rest and recovery to prevent burnout and injury.

Weekly Breakdown

Beginner Track

Designed for those new to running. The focus is on walk-run intervals and gradual increases in running time, with two rest days per week.

Intermediate Track

Designed for runners who have completed a 5K and want to build up to a 10K. The focus is on continuous running with added distance and speed intervals.

Weeks 1-2

Beginners:

- **Monday:** Rest
- **Tuesday:** 20 min walk-run intervals (1 min jog, 3 min walk)
- **Wednesday:** Rest
- **Thursday:** 20 min walk-run intervals (1 min jog, 2 min walk)
- **Friday:** Light stretching or yoga
- **Saturday:** 25 min walk-run intervals (1 min jog, 2 min walk)
- **Sunday:** Rest

Intermediates:

- **Monday:** Rest
- **Tuesday:** 3K easy run
- **Wednesday:** 20 min strength training (focus on legs and core)
- **Thursday:** 4K easy run
- **Friday:** Rest or cross-training (bike or swim)
- **Saturday:** 4K steady pace run
- **Sunday:** Rest

Weeks 3-4

Beginners:

- **Monday:** Rest
- **Tuesday:** 25 min walk-run (2 min jog, 2 min walk)
- **Wednesday:** Light stretching or yoga
- **Thursday:** 30 min walk-run (2 min jog, 1 min walk)
- **Friday:** Rest
- **Saturday:** 3K continuous run or walk-run if needed
- **Sunday:** Rest

Intermediates:

- **Monday:** Rest
- **Tuesday:** 4K easy run with intervals (2 min fast, 2 min easy)
- **Wednesday:** Strength training (focus on legs and core)
- **Thursday:** 5K steady pace
- **Friday:** Rest or cross-training (bike or swim)

- **Saturday:** 5K continuous run
- **Sunday:** Rest

Weeks 5-6

Beginners:

- **Monday:** Rest
- **Tuesday:** 30 min walk-run (3 min jog, 1 min walk)
- **Wednesday:** Light stretching or yoga
- **Thursday:** 3K continuous run
- **Friday:** Rest
- **Saturday:** 4K continuous run
- **Sunday:** Rest

Intermediates:

- **Monday:** Rest
- **Tuesday:** 5K easy run with intervals (3 min fast, 2 min easy)
- **Wednesday:** Strength training (focus on full body)
- **Thursday:** 6K steady pace run
- **Friday:** Rest or cross-training (bike or swim)
- **Saturday:** Tempo run, 5K at goal race pace
- **Sunday:** Rest

Weeks 7-8

Beginners:

- **Monday:** Rest
- **Tuesday:** 4K steady run
- **Wednesday:** Light stretching or yoga
- **Thursday:** 5K continuous run at easy pace
- **Friday:** Rest
- **Saturday:** 5K practice race pace
- **Sunday:** Rest

Intermediates:

- **Monday:** Rest
- **Tuesday:** 6K continuous run with intervals (4 min fast, 2

min easy)
- **Wednesday:** Rest
- **Thursday:** 7K steady pace run
- **Friday:** Cross-training or rest
- **Saturday:** 5K at race pace, focus on pacing control
- **Sunday:** Rest

Additional Tips for Success

Whether you're on the beginner or intermediate track:

- Prioritize rest.
- Listen to your body.
- Stay consistent.
- Both interval and tempo runs are key to building speed and endurance.
- Cross-training adds variety and prevents burnout.
- Adapt these techniques to your pace and progress for the best results.

CHAPTER 4: NUTRITION FOR A 10K RUNNER

The Role of Nutrition in Running Performance

Nutrition plays a crucial role in performance and recovery. Carbs fuel your workouts, proteins aid in muscle repair, and fats provide sustained energy. Through balanced meals, you can support your body's needs, stay energized, and maintain endurance.

Macronutrients Explained

- **Carbohydrates:** Primary source of energy; include whole grains, fruits, and vegetables.
- **Proteins:** Essential for muscle recovery; include lean meats, fish, beans, and tofu.
- **Fats:** Support long-term energy; include avocados, nuts, and olive oil.

Hydration Tips

Hydrate consistently throughout the day. On longer training days, sip water regularly and consider electrolyte options.

Sample Meal Plans

Training Day

Option 1:

- **Breakfast:** Greek yogurt with honey, nuts, and berries
- **Lunch:** Whole-grain wrap with chicken, mixed greens, and hummus
- **Dinner:** Grilled fish, quinoa, and steamed vegetables
- **Snack:** Banana and almond butter

Option 2:

- **Breakfast:** Oatmeal with sliced banana and chia seeds
- **Lunch:** Brown rice bowl with tofu, spinach, and avocado
- **Dinner:** Chicken stir-fry with bell peppers, broccoli, and brown rice
- **Snack:** Apple slices with peanut butter

Option 3:

- **Breakfast:** Smoothie with spinach, almond milk, berries, and protein powder
- **Lunch:** Turkey and avocado on whole-grain toast
- **Dinner:** Baked salmon with sweet potato and green beans
- **Snack:** Handful of nuts and dried fruit

Recovery Day

Option 1:

- **Breakfast:** Scrambled eggs with spinach and whole-grain toast
- **Lunch:** Lentil soup with side salad
- **Dinner:** Baked chicken with roasted sweet potatoes
- **Snack:** Cottage cheese and sliced pineapple

Option 2:

- **Breakfast:** Chia pudding with berries
- **Lunch:** Tuna salad on mixed greens
- **Dinner:** Veggie stir-fry with tofu

- **Snack:** Sliced cucumber and hummus

Option 3:

- **Breakfast:** Smoothie with banana, almond butter, and protein powder
- **Lunch:** Quinoa salad with chickpeas and mixed veggies
- **Dinner:** Grilled shrimp with spaghetti squash
- **Snack:** Greek yogurt with honey

Race Day

Option 1:

- **Pre-Race Breakfast:** Oatmeal with banana and a drizzle of honey
- **Post-Race Meal:** Turkey sandwich on whole-grain bread

Option 2:

- **Pre-Race Breakfast:** Whole-grain toast with almond butter and a sliced apple
- **Post-Race Meal:** Quinoa bowl with grilled chicken

Option 3:

- **Pre-Race Breakfast:** Smoothie with banana, oats, and almond milk
- **Post-Race Meal:** Brown rice and veggie bowl with lean protein

CHAPTER 5: INJURY PREVENTION AND RECOVERY

Common 10K Injuries and How to Avoid Them

Running is a rewarding journey, but it's important to protect your body along the way. Common injuries for runners include shin splints (pain along the front of the lower leg), plantar fasciitis (heel pain caused by inflammation of the tissue on the bottom of the foot), and knee pain (often due to overuse or improper form)—all of which can be minimized with the right approach. Here are some key injury prevention strategies:

Warm-Up and Cool Down

Begin each run with a gentle warm-up. Dynamic stretches, like leg swings and lunges, help loosen muscles and improve range of motion. At the end of each run, spend a few minutes cooling down with slower walking or gentle stretching to relax your muscles and prevent stiffness.

Wear Proper Footwear

Running shoes are your best protection. Visit a specialty running store to get fitted for shoes that suit your gait and running style. Remember to replace your running shoes every 300-500 miles to prevent injuries from worn-out footwear. Shoes with the right amount of cushioning and support can make a world of difference in preventing injuries.

Cross-Train for Strength

Incorporating cross-training into your routine, like cycling, swimming, or strength exercises, supports different muscle groups and gives your running muscles a chance to recover. Strength training that targets the core, glutes, and lower body will help stabilize joints, improve form, and prevent injuries.

Listening to Your Body

One of the most valuable lessons I've learned is to listen to my body. Rest days are just as crucial as training days. They give your muscles and joints time to recover, reducing the risk of overuse injuries. Don't be afraid to take an extra day off if you feel excessively sore or fatigued—this short-term rest can prevent longer-term setbacks.

Pay attention to any unusual discomfort. While it's normal to feel tired or experience mild soreness, sharp or persistent pain, such as shin splints or sudden knee pain, is a red flag. If something doesn't feel right, pause, assess, and consider consulting a healthcare professional. Running should build you up, not wear you down.

Stretching and Foam Rolling

Stretching and foam rolling have been game-changers in my own routine. Stretching helps improve flexibility, while foam rolling massages tight areas, breaking up knots and tension in your muscles. Here's a simple post-run stretching routine to keep your muscles loose and ready for the next run:

- **Hamstring Stretch**: Reach down to touch your toes or gently extend each leg forward, keeping it straight, to stretch your hamstrings.
- **Quad Stretch**: Stand on one leg and pull the opposite foot up towards your glutes. Hold for 20–30 seconds per leg.

- **Hip Flexor Stretch**: In a lunge position, sink your hips forward to stretch the hip flexors.
- **Calf Stretch**: Step one foot forward and push the back heel down, stretching the calf muscles.

Foam rolling is simple and effective. Roll along your calves, quads, IT bands, and back to relieve tension and promote blood flow to those muscles. Spend 1–2 minutes on each muscle group, especially after a long or challenging run. Consistency with these recovery techniques will help you avoid stiffness and recover faster.

CHAPTER 6: STAYING MOTIVATED THROUGHOUT YOUR TRAINING

Overcoming Mental Hurdles

Staying motivated through an 8-week program is key, but motivation naturally ebbs and flows. On some days, lacing up and getting out the door feels effortless; on other days, it's a challenge to find the energy. Remember, this journey is as much about building mental resilience as it is about building physical strength.

On tough days, remind yourself why you started. Picture the moment you cross the finish line, feeling proud and accomplished. Visualize how you'll feel and let that vision carry you forward. Another strategy I use is to set small, manageable goals. When I feel unmotivated, I aim to simply get started—whether that means putting on my running shoes or setting a goal to run for just 10 minutes. More often than not, once I'm out there, I feel motivated to keep going.

When self-doubt creeps in, shift your focus to the progress you've made. Every run, no matter how small, contributes to your goal. Trust in the process and remember that every step forward, even the challenging ones, builds strength and resilience.

The Power of Routine

Establishing a routine can make a huge difference in your consistency. When running becomes part of your daily rhythm, it's easier to stay committed even on low-energy days. Start by setting a regular time to run each day or week. Whether it's early morning or evening, having a routine signals to your body that it's time to run, making it a natural part of your day.

Another effective habit is to lay out your running gear the night before. This small action reduces decision-making in the morning and makes it easier to get going. Building these small habits and sticking to them turns running into an enjoyable and sustainable routine.

Celebrating Small Wins

Every milestone, no matter how small, is worth celebrating. I remember how great it felt when I completed my first 3K without stopping, then my first 5K. Achievements like these build confidence and reinforce your commitment.

Make a list of mini-milestones to celebrate along the way. They could be anything—running your first 4K, finishing your longest run of the week, or reaching the halfway point in the program. Celebrating progress helps you stay positive and keeps the journey enjoyable.

Joining a Running Community

Running with others or joining an online running community can add a new layer of motivation and accountability. Training with friends, family members, or even a local running group gives you support, encouragement, and sometimes a bit of friendly competition. If you prefer solo training, online communities offer encouragement, share tips, and celebrate each other's achievements. Running is a personal journey, but being part of a community can make it even more rewarding.

CHAPTER 7: RACE DAY PREPARATION

My Race-Day Strategy

The big day has arrived! Race day can bring excitement but also nervous energy. Having a well-prepared race-day strategy helps you feel in control and ready for success. Here are the essentials I follow on race day:

- **Plan Your Morning**: Prepare your race-day essentials the night before. Lay out your race outfit, shoes, bib, and any pre-race snacks. Check the weather and prepare layers if needed. Wake up early enough to have a light breakfast and allow time for digestion.
- **Arrive Early**: Give yourself plenty of time to arrive at the starting line, find parking, and get warmed up. Arriving early reduces stress and lets you settle in before the race.
- **Warm Up Gently**: A light warm-up is essential to get your muscles ready without tiring yourself out. Walk or jog lightly for 5–10 minutes, followed by dynamic stretches like leg swings and arm circles.

Mental Tips for Race Day

Race day nerves are natural! Use this nervous energy to your advantage. Think of it as excitement and let it fuel your run. Try taking deep, calming breaths—inhale for four counts, hold for four counts, and exhale for four counts—to help manage nerves and stay focused. When the start signal sounds, remember your pacing. It's easy to get swept up in the excitement and start too fast, but stick to your plan—run at a pace that feels right for you.

Break down the race into manageable sections. Focus on each kilometer rather than thinking about the entire 10K. Each section you complete is a small victory on your way to the finish line. Remind yourself that you've put in the hard work, and trust your training to carry you through.

Visualize crossing the finish line and celebrate your progress every step of the way. Let each completed section give you momentum, knowing that each step brings you closer to achieving your goal.

Post-Race Recovery

After crossing the finish line, it's time to celebrate—but don't skip recovery! Here's my post-race routine to help you recover well:

- **Cool Down**: Slow down gradually with a light jog or walk to bring your heart rate back down.
- **Stretch**: Stretch key muscle groups—hamstrings, calves, quads, and hip flexors. Hold each stretch for at least 30 seconds to release tension.
- **Rehydrate and Refuel**: Drink water or an electrolyte beverage to replenish fluids. Aim to have a carb-protein snack within 30 minutes post-race to kickstart muscle recovery. A banana with peanut butter or a protein smoothie works well.
- **Rest and Reflect**: Take time to relax, stretch out, and reflect on your achievement. Whether it's your first 10K or a milestone in your running journey, finishing a 10K is an accomplishment worth celebrating.

Preparing for Future Runs

Crossing the 10K finish line is a major achievement, but it doesn't have to be the end of your journey. Take some time to celebrate, recover, and assess how you feel. Reflect on what you enjoyed most about training and any areas you'd like to improve.

If you're interested in setting new goals, consider exploring faster times, new race distances, or even different types of running events. Whether you continue with 10Ks or take on new challenges, remember that each run is a step toward building a stronger, more resilient you.

CHAPTER 8: TOP RUNNING WEBSITES AND RESOURCES

Staying Informed and Connected

Running is more than just a physical activity—it's a journey that can be enriched by staying informed and connected to a community of like-minded runners. The following websites, apps, and resources have been invaluable for runners, helping them stay motivated, learn new techniques, and connect with others who share their passion. Here are some top recommendations to keep you informed and inspired:

Runner's World

Runner's World is a go-to source for runners of all levels, offering expert advice on training, injury prevention, gear, nutrition, and more through articles, videos, and community discussions. With a mix of science-based articles, personal stories, and practical tips, it's a well-rounded resource for anyone looking to improve their running knowledge.

Strava

Strava has become one of the most popular apps among runners and other athletes. Known as the "social network for athletes," Strava lets you track your runs, analyze performance metrics, and share your progress with friends. You can also join running challenges, explore routes, and connect with the global running community.

MapMyRun

MapMyRun by Under Armour is another excellent app that helps you map out and track your routes. It includes stats on distance, pace, elevation, and calories burned. MapMyRun is especially helpful if you like discovering new routes or want to compare different runs over time.

Hal Higdon's Training Programs

Hal Higdon is a respected running coach whose training programs are widely used and appreciated by runners of all levels. His website offers a variety of structured training plans, such as a beginner 10K plan, which provides a clear roadmap for those new to running longer distances. His website offers free, structured training plans for various distances, including the 10K, with clear guidance on pacing and mileage.

Podcasts: "The Morning Shakeout" and "Marathon Training Academy"

Listening to running podcasts can provide insight, motivation, and fresh perspectives on training and mental resilience. "The Morning Shakeout" offers interviews with runners, coaches, and industry experts, while "Marathon Training Academy" covers a wide range of running topics, from motivation to race preparation.

YouTube Channels: The Running Channel and Global Triathlon Network (GTN)

For visual learners, YouTube offers helpful resources on technique, stretching, cross-training, and more. Channels like The Running Channel and GTN provide instructional videos, running tips, and motivation to keep you engaged and improving.

These resources can help you deepen your understanding of

running, connect with others, and stay motivated throughout your training. Whether you're looking to improve your form, track your progress, or simply get inspired, these tools provide the support you need to keep moving forward.

CHAPTER 9: RACE DAY PREPARATION

My Race-Day Strategy

When race day arrives, having a strategy in place will help you feel prepared, calm, and focused. Over time, I've developed a race-day routine that helps me start strong and stay steady through every kilometer. Here's my step-by-step guide to ensure you're ready to go:

The Night Before

Begin preparation the night before to minimize morning stress. Lay out your race gear, including clothes, shoes, bib (if provided in advance), and any nutrition you'll need. Double-check the weather forecast to see if extra layers or rain protection are necessary. I also make a light, carb-focused dinner—like pasta or rice with a lean protein—to fuel up without feeling too full.

Get Enough Sleep

It's common to feel a bit nervous the night before a race, but try to go to bed early to rest. Even if it takes a while to fall asleep, a calm evening helps you feel more energized in the morning. If nerves make sleep difficult, don't stress—excitement and adrenaline will give you the boost you need on race day.

Race Morning

On race day, have a light breakfast about 2–3 hours before the race. A banana with peanut butter or a small bowl of oatmeal with honey are great options that provide quick energy without causing digestive discomfort. Hydrate well in the hours leading up to the race but avoid excessive water intake right before the start to avoid discomfort.

Arrive Early

Give yourself extra time to arrive, find parking, and get settled at the race venue. I aim to arrive at least an hour before the race begins, which allows time for warming up, checking in, and mentally preparing without feeling rushed.

Warm-Up

A gentle warm-up is essential to prepare your muscles. I start with a 5–10 minute light jog or brisk walk, followed by dynamic stretches such as leg swings, lunges, and arm circles. This routine increases blood flow and loosens up any tight muscles, reducing the risk of injury.

Mental Tips for Race Day

Race day often brings a mix of excitement and nerves. Embrace the energy and stay focused on your plan. Here are a few mental strategies I use to stay calm and centered:

Channel the Excitement

It's normal to feel nervous, but try to reframe it as excitement. Remind yourself of all the training you've done, and visualize crossing the finish line. This positive anticipation helps you stay focused and energized.

Pace Yourself

It's tempting to start fast with the crowd, but I always remind myself to hold back and stick to my planned pace. A steady start helps prevent burnout and gives you the energy to pick up speed later in the race if you feel strong.

Break It Down

Instead of focusing on the full 10K, break the race into smaller sections. Concentrate on reaching each kilometer or landmark. Celebrating these mini-victories along the way helps keep motivation high and makes the race feel more manageable.

Post-Race Recovery

Crossing the finish line is an incredible feeling, but recovery is essential to avoid post-race fatigue and soreness. Here's my post-race routine to help you recover well and celebrate your accomplishment:

Cool Down

After finishing, gradually slow down with a light jog or walk for 5-10 minutes to bring your heart rate back down.

Stretch

Take a few minutes to stretch key muscle groups, focusing on the hamstrings, quads, calves, and hip flexors. Holding each stretch for at least 30 seconds helps release tension and prevent stiffness.

Rehydrate and Refuel

Drink water or a sports drink to replenish lost fluids. Aim to eat a snack with both carbs and protein within 30 minutes to kickstart muscle recovery. A banana with peanut butter or a protein smoothie works well.

Celebrate Your Success

Completing a 10K is a huge accomplishment. Take time to reflect on your journey, enjoy the achievement, and thank yourself for the hard work you put in.

CHAPTER 10: SAMPLE TRAINING LOGS AND TRACKING TOOLS

Tracking Your 10K Progress

Tracking your progress is a fantastic way to stay motivated and see how far you've come. Recording each run helps you analyze improvements, monitor your pace, and make adjustments to your training plan. Here's a simple tracking log template to help you document each run and stay consistent.

10K Training Log Template

Below is a sample log that you can use to track the essential details of each run, including the date, distance, duration, pace, and personal notes. Noting how you felt during each run can help identify patterns, and it's a great way to celebrate your progress at the end of each week.

Date	Distance	Duration	Pace	Notes/Feelings
01/01/2023	4K	30 min	7:30/km	Felt strong, enjoyed the pace
01/02/2023	5K	38 min	7:40/km	Slight knee soreness, took it easy

| 01/04/2023 | 6K | 45 min | 7:30/km | Great run, weather was perfect |

Customize this log to suit your needs. Over time, tracking gives you a clear picture of your progress and helps you appreciate the distance you've covered.

Recommended Tracking Tools

For those who prefer digital tracking, these tools make it easy to monitor and analyze your runs:

Strava

Strava is a popular app that tracks your routes, pace, and distance. It also connects you with a global running community, making it ideal for accountability and motivation. Strava's performance metrics and analysis tools help you visualize progress over time.

Nike Run Club

Nike Run Club provides tracking features along with guided runs, coaching, and community support. It's beginner-friendly and helps keep you motivated through in-app challenges and personalized plans.

MapMyRun

MapMyRun allows you to plan and save routes, track your pace and distance, and monitor elevation changes. It's ideal if you like exploring new areas or trying out different running paths.

Garmin Connect

If you use a Garmin device, Garmin Connect offers in-depth tracking, including heart rate, pace, and performance insights. The app syncs with Garmin watches, making it a powerful tool for data-driven runners.

Celebrating Progress and Setting New Goals

Tracking your runs is more than just logging numbers—it's a way to celebrate each step forward. At the end of each week, review your log and recognize the progress you've made. Whether you hit a new distance, improved your pace, or simply felt great on a run, each entry is a win.

As you near the end of your 10K training journey, use your progress log to reflect on your achievements and set new goals. Consider aiming for a faster 10K, a new race distance, or even setting a monthly mileage target. Each goal is a step toward continued growth and the joy that running brings.

CHAPTER 11: ADVANCED TIPS FOR FUTURE 10K RUNNERS

Beyond the Finish Line: Setting New Goals

Crossing the 10K finish line is a remarkable achievement, but for many runners, it's just the beginning. Setting new goals helps keep the excitement alive and provides a sense of purpose, making each run even more rewarding. Completing a 10K not only builds physical stamina but also ignites a passion for further challenges. Whether you're interested in improving your time, aiming for a longer distance, or simply continuing to run for health and enjoyment, this chapter provides some advanced tips to guide you in your next steps.

Improving Your 10K Time

If you're ready to take on a faster 10K, structured speed training is key. It helps improve both cardiovascular capacity and muscle efficiency, allowing you to run faster and more efficiently. Here are a few methods that have helped me and other runners build speed and shave time off our races:

- **Intervals**: Interval training combines short bursts of high-speed running with periods of rest. For example, try running 400 meters at a fast pace (about 80-90% of your maximum effort), followed by 200 meters of light jogging or walking. Repeat this sequence 6–8 times. Interval training improves

both speed and endurance, helping you run faster and longer over time.
- **Tempo Runs**: A tempo run is a sustained run at a challenging pace that you can maintain for 15–30 minutes. Tempo runs help build stamina and teach your body to maintain speed over longer distances. To start, aim to run at a pace that's "comfortably hard"—challenging but manageable—and gradually extend the duration.
- **Hill Training**: Adding hills to your routine builds leg strength, increases aerobic capacity, and improves running efficiency. Find a hill with a moderate incline and aim to run up at a steady pace, then jog or walk back down. Repeat for several rounds. This will prepare you for races with elevation changes and make flat courses feel easier.

Considering Longer Distances

If you've enjoyed the 10K training process and feel ready for a new challenge, a half marathon might be a great goal to set your sights on. Transitioning to a half marathon can help you improve your endurance and mental toughness, pushing you to achieve even greater milestones. A half marathon is a 21.1K race, and while it's a significant increase in distance, it's achievable with the right preparation. Transitioning to a half marathon builds on your 10K base, so you already have a strong foundation.

To get started, gradually increase your weekly mileage, focusing on long runs that build endurance. Aim to add 1–2K to your longest run each week until you reach around 16K. This prepares your body and mind for the demands of a longer race, giving you confidence as you approach race day.

Exploring Trail Running and Cross-Training

For a refreshing change of scenery and an added challenge, consider exploring trail running. Running on trails requires balance, coordination, and agility, as you navigate uneven terrain. Trails offer a mental escape and the chance to connect with nature, making it an excellent way to keep running exciting. Start with shorter, local trails and gradually work up to longer, more challenging routes.

Cross-training can also enhance your running performance. Swimming, cycling, and yoga improve overall fitness while giving your running muscles a break. Yoga, in particular, is beneficial for building flexibility and balance, which can improve your stride and reduce the risk of injury.

Setting Personal Challenges and Celebrating Wins

Running is a journey, and setting personal challenges keeps it fulfilling. For example, you could try running a new route, aiming for a specific weekly mileage, or completing a run in a set time. Try aiming for a specific number of kilometers each month, signing up for local races, or challenging yourself to run a new distance or location each week. Tracking these accomplishments, even if they're not race-related, helps you stay motivated and gives you a sense of pride and progress.

Celebrate each new milestone, no matter how big or small. Every time you achieve something new, you're becoming a stronger, more resilient runner. Embrace the challenges and keep moving forward, one run at a time.

CHAPTER 12: CONCLUSION AND NEXT STEPS

Reflecting on Your Journey

Congratulations on completing your first 10K training journey! This is a moment to celebrate, reflect, and recognize the commitment you made to yourself. Whether it was pushing through early morning runs, dealing with unexpected setbacks, or overcoming the challenge of staying motivated, your dedication has truly paid off. Completing a 10K is no small feat, and whether it's your first time running this distance or a step up from a shorter race, you've achieved something incredible.

Take a moment to think back to where you started: the early days of training, the challenges you faced, and the progress made with each step. Running has a unique way of teaching us resilience, focus, and patience. Pushing through challenging runs teaches the value of mental strength and perseverance. Moments like these remind us how running builds both our physical and mental endurance. Every mile you ran has contributed to a stronger body, a sharper mind, and a deeper understanding of your own potential.

Carrying Forward the Lessons of Running

The lessons you've learned during this journey don't end here.

Consistency, mental resilience, and achieving goals are lifelong skills that can be applied to many areas of your life. Whether it's tackling a challenging project at work, managing personal relationships, or pursuing a new hobby, the dedication and perseverance you've built through running will help you succeed. Running has likely become more than just a fitness activity; it's a lifestyle, a source of strength, and a way to connect with yourself.

As you look forward, remember that the habits you've built and the milestones you've reached can support you in all areas of life. Whether it's in work, personal challenges, or future fitness goals, the dedication you showed here is something you can apply wherever you choose.

Embracing New Goals and Challenges

Running offers endless possibilities for growth and adventure. You might decide to improve your 10K time, aim for a longer distance, or take on new terrains like trail running. Each goal is an opportunity to continue discovering your potential and exploring what you're capable of achieving.

The 10K is a meaningful accomplishment, but it's also important to take the time to celebrate this achievement before moving on to even greater challenges. Acknowledging your progress will help you maintain balance and motivation as you set your sights on new goals. Take a moment to set a specific new goal—whether it's running a faster 10K, tackling a half marathon, or exploring trail running. Setting a clear target will help you take the next step with confidence. Keep setting goals, stay curious about what's possible, and don't hesitate to try new things. The road ahead is full of potential, and the journey of a runner is one that grows richer with every mile.

Parting Words of Encouragement

As you move forward, hold on to the sense of accomplishment you feel today. You've proven that you're capable of dedication, resilience, and strength. Remember that time when you had to push through a tough training session despite feeling drained? That moment showed your ability to persevere, and it's a reminder of just how resilient you can be. The experiences you've gained through running will always be there, reminding you that you have the power to reach your goals. These lessons can also be applied to other areas of life, like tackling challenges at work, strengthening personal relationships, or pursuing new opportunities with confidence.

Set your sights on your next challenge, whether it's another 10K, a half marathon, or simply running for joy and health. I wish you success, fulfillment, and happiness as you continue your journey. Remember that every run is a step forward, and each finish line, no matter the distance, is a new beginning. Celebrate every bit of progress, no matter how small, because each step brings you closer to your goals.

Keep running, stay inspired, and enjoy every mile ahead. Share your journey with others or join a running community for added support and motivation.

SHARE YOUR THOUGHTS!

Thank you for joining me on this journey through **Run Your First 10K: A Step-by-Step Beginner's Guide from Couch to Confident Finisher**. I hope this book has inspired and guided you toward achieving your running goals.

If you found this book helpful, I'd truly appreciate it if you could take a moment to leave a review on Amazon. Your feedback helps other runners discover the book and begin their own journeys.

A quick rating or comment on what you found useful makes a big difference. To leave your review, simply visit the book's page on Amazon and click "Write a Review."

Thank you for your time, your support, and for being part of this amazing running community! If you enjoyed this book, please consider sharing it with your friends or running groups to help grow our community even further.

Tomasz Tomaszewski

Printed in Great Britain
by Amazon